Wandsworth

Monstrous limericks   27

D1610851

Written and illustrated by Shoo Rayner

QUESTIONS, QUESTIONS

What should you do if a monster bashes your front door down?
Run out of the back door as quickly as you can.

Did you hear what happened when the girl monster met the boy monster?
They fell in love at first fright.

"My new boyfriend took me to see a scary monster film last night."
"Wow! What was it like?"
"Ooh! About three metres tall with wild green hair and crazy, bulging pop-out eyes!"
"No! Not your boyfriend – what was the film like?"

What do you say to a three-headed monster?
"Hello, hello, hello."

What did Doctor Who say when he saw a gang of monsters walking over the hill?
"There's a gang of monsters walking over the hill!"

What did Doctor Who say when he saw a gang of monsters walking over the hill in sunglasses?
Nothing, he didn't recognise them!

How does a monster
count to seventeen?
On its fingers!

Why did the one-armed
monster cross the road?
*To get to the
second-hand shop!*

only
one
careful
owner.

Why did the monster
give up boxing?
*It didn't want to spoil
its lovely good looks.*

What do you call a
monster with five ears?
Eerie!

What do you call a kind,
good-looking, considerate,
generous, thoughtful monster?
Rubbish!

Why did the flaky
monster visit the doctor?
*Because it wasn't
peeling very well.*

What would you do if you saw a gang of
monsters walking down your road?
Hope they were going to a fancy-dress party.

MONSTER MUNCH

What do monsters
eat for breakfast?
Dreaded Wheat!

Which day do monsters
eat people?
Chewsday!

What do sea monsters eat?
Fish and ships!

Why did the monster have a terrible tummy ache?
It had eaten someone who disagreed with it.

How do you know if a monster's been in the fridge?
There are footprints in the butter!

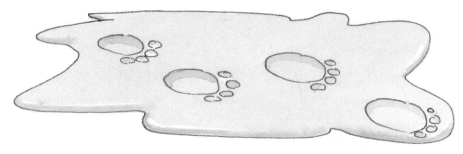

What is a monster's favourite food?
Kate and Sidney pie.

7

"What's the difference between a monster and a banana?"
"I don't know."
"Well, you won't last very long!"

What did the polite werewolf say?

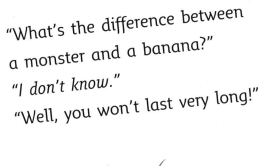

I'm pleased to eat you!

What did the other polite werewolf say?

It's been nice gnawing you!

FAMILY MATTERS

"Mummy, Mummy, can I bring a friend home for tea?"

"Of course, sweetie. Put him in the fridge and we'll have him later."

"Dad, that monster over there rolled her eyes at me!"

"Well, son, you just roll them right back again."

"Mum, did you hear about the monster ballet?"

"It's called Swamp Lake."

What has three heads, three arms and five legs?

A monster with spare parts.

What did Daddy Bigfoot do when he got thirsty?

He put on tap shoes.

Why are monster shoes so rude?
Because they stick their tongues out!

"You've got beautiful eyes!"
*"Thank you. They were a birthday present
from my mum."*

KNOCK, KNOCK ...

Knock, knock ...
Who's there?
Bernadette.
Bernadette who?
Bernadette my teddy bear!

Knock, knock ...
Who's there?
Ghosts go.
Ghosts go who?
No! Ghosts go "Woooh!"

Knock, knock ...
Who's there?
Dwayne.
Dwayne who?
Dwayne the lake, the monster's got to be down there!

Knock, knock ...
Who's there?
Freddie.
Freddie who?
Freddie or not – here I come!

13

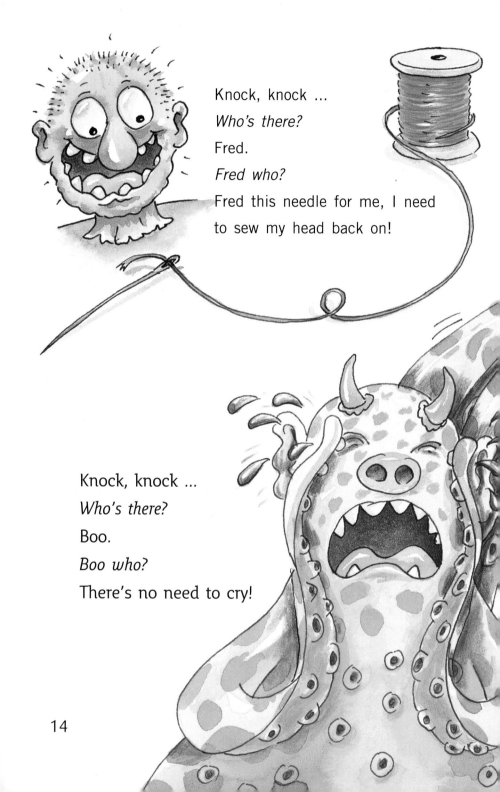

Knock, knock ...
Who's there?
Fred.
Fred who?
Fred this needle for me, I need to sew my head back on!

Knock, knock ...
Who's there?
Boo.
Boo who?
There's no need to cry!

14

Knock, knock ...

Who's there?

Sarah.

Sarah who?

Sarah monster living here?

... and finally

What do you do if a green monster is knocking on your door?

Wait until it's ripe!

FRANKENSTEIN'S MONSTER

What did the monster say when Frankenstein zapped him with ten million volts of electricity?

Wow! That was great!

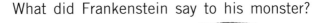

What did Frankenstein say to his monster?

Get a life!

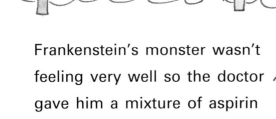

Frankenstein's monster wasn't feeling very well so the doctor gave him a mixture of aspirin and glue.

He had a splitting headache!

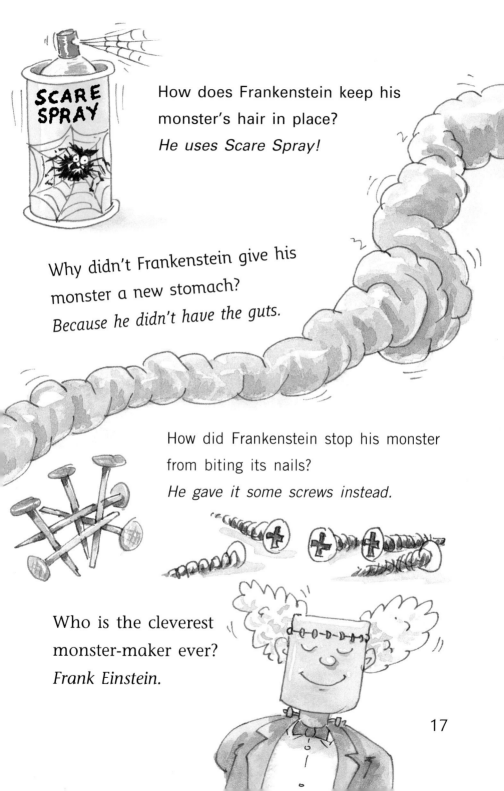

How does Frankenstein keep his monster's hair in place?
He uses Scare Spray!

Why didn't Frankenstein give his monster a new stomach?
Because he didn't have the guts.

How did Frankenstein stop his monster from biting its nails?
He gave it some screws instead.

Who is the cleverest monster-maker ever?
Frank Einstein.

What did Frankenstein say when he saw his monster had a cucumber in his right ear, a banana in his left ear, and a carrot up its nose?

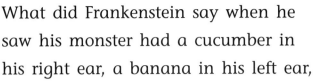

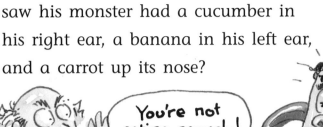

You're not eating properly!

Doctor, doctor, I get a sharp pain in my eye every time I drink.

Try taking the spoon out of your mug!

How did Frankenstein stop his monster's nose from running?

He stuck his foot out and tripped it up!

MONSTER BOOKS

MONSTER MYTHS

Why did Cyclops give up teaching?
He needed more than one pupil.

Why did Cyclops always fight with his brother?
Because they could never see eye to eye!

Why did Cyclops wear sunglasses in the rain?
To protect himself from umbrellas.

What did the big dragon say to the
little dragon?

"Smoking is really bad for you!"

What did the dragon say when it saw
the knight in shining armour?

Yummy, tinned food!

What sort of aeroplane is like a dragon?

A Spitfire!

DID YOU KNOW?

What's a monster's favourite party game?
Swallow my leader!

How can you contact
the Loch Ness monster?
Drop it a line.

Why did the monster sit on the
little boy?
Because it wanted to play squash!

Why did the monster
wear sunglasses?
*It didn't want anyone
to recognise it!*

22

What goes "Ha, ha, bonk"?
A *monster laughing its head off.*

What goes "Ha, ha, bonk, bonk"?
A *monster laughing both its heads off!*

Why was the monster embarrassed when it was asked to take its mask off at the fancy dress party?
It wasn't wearing one!

How can you tell if there is a monster in your bedroom?
It'll have an "M" on its dressing gown.

23

Why did the invisible man look in the mirror? *To check he wasn't there!*

What do you call a monster with a spade? *Doug.*

What did the werewolf who turned into a boy say?

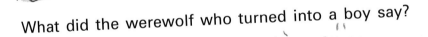

I used to be a werewolf but I'm all right now-ow-owww!

MONSTER STORIES

A monster went up to an ice-cream van and asked for
a choc-ice.

The ice-cream seller was surprised, but thought he would
try and cheat the monster.

"That'll be a bag of gold, please," he said.

The monster pulled out a bag of gold and paid.

The ice-cream seller said, "We don't get many monsters
like you round here."

*The monster replied, "At a bag of gold for a choc-ice,
I'm not surprised!"*

A policeman saw a man shaking something over the road.

The man explained that it was special dust to keep monsters away.

"But there aren't any monsters around here!" said the policeman.

"I know," said the man ... "This stuff really works, doesn't it?"

26

MONSTROUS LIMERICKS

There once was a monster called Fred,
Who used to eat onions in bed.
His mother said, "Sonny,
It's not very funny.
Why don't you eat people instead?"

A sea monster saw a big tanker,
Bit a hole in her side and then sank her.
He swallowed the crew,
In a minute or two,
And then picked his teeth with the anchor!

27

MUM xx

A monster called Terrible Ed,
Used to sleep in a specially built bed.
It was three metres high,
So that Eddy could lie,
With the ceiling on top of his head.

A ghostly young monster called Paul
Once went to a fancy-dress ball.
To shock every guest
He went there undressed,
But no one could see him at all.

🐾 Ideas for guided reading 🐾

Learning objectives: compare forms or types of humour, e.g. by exploring, collecting and categorising form or type of humour; secure knowledge of question marks and exclamation marks in reading, understanding their purpose and use appropriately in own writing; choose and prepare poems or stories for performance, identifying appropriate expression, tone, volume and use of voices and other sounds

Curriculum links: ICT: Combining text and graphics

Interest words: considerate, dreaded, werewolf, electricity, volts, aspirin, abominable, embarrassed

Getting started

This book can be read over two or more guided reading sessions.

- Select one or two jokes from the book and share them with the group. Ask them to talk about what makes jokes funny.

- Draw attention to the 'knock knock' joke in the blurb and ask the group to say how this kind of joke works.

- Examine the contents page and show how the book is organised into topics and types of jokes. The group could choose a chapter to read first.

- Turn to that page and briefly discuss the layout of the page, showing the children how illustrations break up the text and help guide the reader through the jokes.

Reading and responding

- As they take turns to tell each other the jokes, check that they are using questioning voices and good expression for the punch lines. Ensure that they observe punctuation such as commas and exclamation marks.

- Before moving on, ask them to return to the contents page. As a group discuss the meaning of the word *myths* and *limericks* and check that they know about Frankenstein.